ABUNDANT TRUTH INTERNATIONAL MINISTRIES

Abundant Truth Spiritual Gifts Series

MASTERING THE GIFTS OF SERVICE

Exploring the Roman and Corinthian Endowments

Roderick Levi Evans

Published by Abundant Truth Publishing
P.O. Box 126
Camden, NC 27921
Web: www.abundantpublishing.net
Email: abundantpublishing@gmail.com

Printed U.S.A.

Front & Back Cover Designs by Abundant Truth Publishing
All rights reserved.
Free-use Cover Image

Abundant Truth Publishing is a ministry of **Abundant Truth International Ministries.** The primary mission of ATI Ministries is to equip the Body of Christ with tools necessary to defend and contend for the truth of the Christian faith. Jesus Christ came to bear witness of the truth and ATI Ministries is a modern-day extension of His commission (John 18:37).

Abundant Truth Spiritual Gifts Series – Mastering the Gifts of Service
©2024 Abundant Truth Publishing
All Rights Reserved
ISBN13: 978-1-60141-629-2

Printed in the United States of America

Unless otherwise indicated, all of the scripture quotations are taken from the *Authorized King James Version* of the Bible. Scripture quotations marked with NIV are taken from the *New International Version* of the Bible. Scripture quotations marked with NASV are taken from the *New American Standard Version* of the Bible. Scripture quotations marked with Amplified are taken from the *Amplified Bible*

Contents

Introduction

Chapter 1 – Ministering/Helps   1

The Ability to Serve   *3*

The Attitude of Service   *4*

Chapter 2 – Teaching   9

Gifted Endowment   *11*

Gifted Instructors   *12*

Chapter 3 – Exhortation   15

Gifted Encouragers   *17*

Gifted Motivators   *18*

Chapter 4 – Giving   23

Wise Giver   *25*

Contents (cont.)

Generous Giver   26

Chapter 5 – Ruleth/Governments   31
The Broader Application   33
The Broader Expression   34

Chapter 6 – Showing Mercy   39
Christ's Compassion   41
Christ-like Exhorter   42

Chapter 7 – Dreams and Visions   45
The Dreaming Disciple   47
The Interpreting Disciple   50

Bibliography   55

Introduction

The promise of the Father was the fulfillment of God's prophecy through Joel. One result of the Spirit's coming would be prophetic revelation and the manifestation of dreams and visions. We discover from Paul's discussions of the gifts in I Corinthian 12 that the Spirit is responsible for the dispersion of the gifts. In the Abundant Truth Spiritual Gifts Series, we will examine the gifts of the Spirit and their operations in the New Testament Church.

In this publication:

Aside from the nine gifts of the Spirit listed in Corinthians, Paul in two other passages mentioned other gifts. Often times, they are excluded when the gifts of the Spirit are mentioned.

In addition, in Romans, Paul lists other ministries and/or gifts of the Spirit along with familiar ones. From these two passages, we discover these other gifts of the Spirit:

So we, being many, are one body in Christ, and every one members one of another. Having then gifts differing according to the grace that is given to us, whether prophecy, let us prophesy according to the proportion of our faith; Or ministry, let us wait on our ministering: or he that teacheth, on teaching; Or he that exhorteth, on exhortation: he that giveth, let him do it with simplicity; he that ruleth, with diligence; he that showeth mercy, with cheerfulness. (Romans 12:5-8)

And God hath set some in the church, first apostles, secondarily prophets, thirdly teachers, after that miracles, then the gifts of healings, helps, governments, diversities of tongues. (I Corinthians 12:28)

In this publication, we will discuss the ancillary or "other gifts" of the Spirit which are addressed in brief in Paul's letter to the Romans and I Corinthians 12. It is our prayer that believers will develop an appreciation for these gifts.

MASTERING THE GIFTS OF SERVICE

-Chapter 1-

Ministering/Helps

MASTERING THE GIFTS OF SERVICE

MASTERING THE GIFTS OF SERVICE

When the scripture is quoted from Romans, "let us wait on our ministering," many feel that Paul is referring to a call to the ministry.

The Ability to Serve

In scripture, to minister means 'to serve.' Paul was instructing the believers then that before they just jump into service, no matter what type, they should wait.

Since Paul is referring to service, it is our belief that this was also what he was referring to in Corinthians when he said

MASTERING THE GIFTS OF SERVICE

"helps." God has placed individuals in the Church who will serve and aid in whatever capacity.

The Attitude of Service

I Corinthians 12 said that God set those with the gift or ministry of helps in the Church. It is a God-given ability. People who serve are anointed and sent by God, even as those called to the ministry.

Believers who have this gift usually work well on the pastor's aid, usher board, deacon board, tape ministry, bus ministry,

MASTERING THE GIFTS OF SERVICE

hospitality committee, and the like.

MASTERING THE GIFTS OF SERVICE

MASTERING THE GIFTS OF SERVICE

Notes:

MASTERING THE GIFTS OF SERVICE

MASTERING THE GIFTS OF SERVICE

-Chapter 2-

Teaching

MASTERING THE GIFTS OF SERVICE

MASTERING THE GIFTS OF SERVICE

Paul lists teaching as a gift of the spirit. As with prophecy, individuals may have the gift of prophecy but are not prophets or prophetesses.

Gifted Endowment

It is the same with teaching. There are individuals who are gifted to teach but are not called to the office of the teacher. These individuals are gifted to teach the word in various formats.

They have the ability to present the word in a way that is orderly and understandable.

MASTERING THE GIFTS OF SERVICE

Gifted Instructors

Those who have this gift are usually Sunday school teachers, vacation bible school instructors, youth workers, seminary teachers and professors. They work in the teaching aspects of the church.

MASTERING THE GIFTS OF SERVICE

Notes:

MASTERING THE GIFTS OF SERVICE

MASTERING THE GIFTS OF SERVICE

-Chapter 3-

Exhortation

MASTERING THE GIFTS OF SERVICE

MASTERING THE GIFTS OF SERVICE

The gift of exhortation is commonly found in the Church. Individuals with this gift have the ability to stir the people of God.

Gifted Encouragers

They have the ability to motivate the people of God to change and action whether in praise and worship or in their walks with God.

Though we are to exhort and encourage one another, some are gifted in this area. Being in their presence is like taking a bath. You leave from them

MASTERING THE GIFTS OF SERVICE

uplifted and strengthened.

Gifted Motivators

People who have this gift are usually praise and worship leaders and moderators over services. Individual believers possessing this gift will give powerful testimonies.

Others will be behind the scenes. They are those individuals who can encourage you and strengthen you over the phone or while in conversation.

Another error that has occurred in the Church is that those with this gift are

MASTERING THE GIFTS OF SERVICE

sometimes mistaken to be evangelists since they can exhort and get people excited. Often times others push them into ministry and their ministry is weak and it lacks substance because they are trying to operate in the wrong calling.

MASTERING THE GIFTS OF SERVICE

MASTERING THE GIFTS OF SERVICE

Notes:

_____

_____

_____

_____

_____

_____

_____

_____

MASTERING THE GIFTS OF SERVICE

MASTERING THE GIFTS OF SERVICE

-Chapter 4-

Giving

MASTERING THE GIFTS OF SERVICE

MASTERING THE GIFTS OF SERVICE

In the Word, we are all instructed to give and give liberally. But, Paul lists giving as one of the gifts that individuals possess.

Wise Giver

They that have this gift must not only have the faith to give, but also **wisdom**.

> *But this I say, He which soweth sparingly shall reap also sparingly; and he which soweth bountifully shall reap also bountifully. (2 Corinthians 9:6)*

MASTERING THE GIFTS OF SERVICE

This is why he instructed those with the gift of giving to do it with simplicity. This is so they will not become puffed up. Those with this gift must possess a selfless mentality, or they will run the risk of giving for vainglory.

Generous Giver

The person with this gift will not only share their finances, but their time effort and personal resources. They keep in mind this proverb,

> *A generous man will be blessed, for he shares his bread with the*

MASTERING THE GIFTS OF SERVICE

poor. (Proverbs 22:9 BSB)

MASTERING THE GIFTS OF SERVICE

MASTERING THE GIFTS OF SERVICE

Notes:

MASTERING THE GIFTS OF SERVICE

MASTERING THE GIFTS OF SERVICE

-Chapter 5-

Ruleth/Governments

MASTERING THE GIFTS OF SERVICE

MASTERING THE GIFTS OF SERVICE

Paul lists "he that ruleth" and "governments" as gifts. It is our belief here that when Paul spoke of "he that rules" in Romans, it is in conjunction to "governments" set in the Church by God.

The Broader Application

When we speak of rules and governments in the Church it is only believed to refer to pastors and the bishops. Though this is true, there is a broader expression of this gift.

Aside from pastors and elders, individuals in the body also have the gift to rule or governments. Usually these individuals serve as the head of boards and departments in the Church. We have seen many in the Church who are not called to the ministry yet possess God-given leadership skills and qualities.

The Broader Expression

Believers operating with this gift usually serve as youth leaders and counselors; they are heads of men and women departments, and the like. They will have the ability to gather believers together to accomplish goals. They will

MASTERING THE GIFTS OF SERVICE

have vision and insight for the department that they are leading. They have both administrative and leadership skills while serving the vision of their pastor or leader.

MASTERING THE GIFTS OF SERVICE

MASTERING THE GIFTS OF SERVICE

Notes:

_____

_____

_____

_____

_____

_____

_____

_____

MASTERING THE GIFTS OF SERVICE

MASTERING THE GIFTS OF SERVICE

-Chapter 6-

Showing Mercy

MASTERING THE GIFTS OF SERVICE

MASTERING THE GIFTS OF SERVICE

We are exhorted in the scriptures to love and be merciful. Yet, God has gifted individuals who can demonstrate love and compassion in a greater measure than others.

Christ's Compassion

We have all met individuals who know just what to say and do in a bad situation.

And let us consider one another to provoke unto love and to good works. (Hebrews 10:24)

We ought to give praise for those

MASTERING THE GIFTS OF SERVICE

individuals who possess this gift.

Christ-like Exhorter

Believers with this gift will often times have the gift of exhortation in addition. They will know how to empathize with you when you are hurt, lonely, confused, or angry and will know what to say to help you keep progressing.

MASTERING THE GIFTS OF SERVICE

Notes:

_____

_____

_____

_____

_____

_____

_____

_____

MASTERING THE GIFTS OF SERVICE

-Chapter 7-

Dreams and Visions

MASTERING THE GIFTS OF SERVICE

MASTERING THE GIFTS OF SERVICE

Along with our study of the gifts, we shall also look at two other "gifts." They are Dreams and Visions.

The Dreaming Disciple

Some believers consistently have dreams and visions. Therefore, they should be respected as gifts from God.

And it shall come to pass in the last days, saith God, I will pour out of my Spirit upon all flesh; and your sons and daughters shall prophesy, and your young men shall see VISIONS, and your old men shall DREAM

MASTERING THE GIFTS OF SERVICE

dreams. (Joel 2:28 Emphasis mine)

It is not uncommon for God to speak to believers occasionally in dreams and visions. Scripture shows us that God used dreams and visions to communicate with His people.

We also find in scripture there are certain individuals whom God chose to speak to regularly in dreams and in visions.

Even in the Old Testament there were individuals recognized for their ability to dream.

MASTERING THE GIFTS OF SERVICE

If there arise among you a prophet, or a DREAMER OF DREAMS, and giveth thee a sign or a wonder... Deuteronomy13:1; Emphasis mine)

It was understood that God spoke to individuals regularly in dreams and visions. We must learn to hear God speaking to us in this manner at night. If you dream regularly, God may be trying to establish communication with you while you are asleep.

In addition, not every vision has to be an open vision; most visions we see in

MASTERING THE GIFTS OF SERVICE

our spirit. We must learn not to reject them as from God.

The Interpreting Disciple

Not only are individuals given to dreams and visions, but also some are gifted to interpret dreams and visions. If you dream or see visions, pray that God will give you understanding.

If you are gifted in one of the aforementioned "other" gifts, please do not think that these gifts are secondary to those in I Corinthians 12:1-8. You will find that the other gifts come and go, but

MASTERING THE GIFTS OF SERVICE

these gifts are needed at all times in the Church. Again, if you are unsure of your gift, do not let the enemy trick you. Talk to your leaders, they will help and direct you.

MASTERING THE GIFTS OF SERVICE

MASTERING THE GIFTS OF SERVICE

Notes:

MASTERING THE GIFTS OF SERVICE

Bibliography

Evans, Roderick L. Kingdom Practice, Power, and Principle Writers Club Press. Lincoln, NE, c2002

Lockman Foundation. Comparative Study Bible. Zondervan Publishing House. Grand Rapids, MI, c1984

Tucker, Ron & Hufton, Rick. God's Plan For Christian Service. Grace Church. St. Louis, MO, c1987

MASTERING THE GIFTS OF SERVICE

The Bible Library. The Bible Library CD Rom Disc. Ellis Enterprises Incorporated, (c) 1988 – 2000. 4205 McAuley Blvd., Suite 385, Oklahoma City, OK 73120. All Rights Reserved.

MASTERING THE GIFTS OF SERVICE

Notes:

MASTERING THE GIFTS OF SERVICE

MASTERING THE GIFTS OF SERVICE

Notes:

MASTERING THE GIFTS OF SERVICE

MASTERING THE GIFTS OF SERVICE

Notes:

_____

_____

_____

_____

_____

_____

_____

_____

MASTERING THE GIFTS OF SERVICE

www.ingramcontent.com/pod-product-compliance
Lightning Source LLC
Chambersburg PA
CBHW050344010526
44119CB00049B/690